PLANTING A PARADISE

Published by -
Truran,
Croft Prince,
Mount Hawke,
Truro
Cornwall TR4 8EE

Printed by -
R. Booth at the
Troutbeck Press,
Antron Hill,
Mabe, Penryn.
Cornwall TR10 9HH

ISBN 1 85022 151 0 (Cased)
ISBN 1 85022 152 9 (Paperback)

this is just the beginning . . . . . .

THE BIG BUILD .

that's what all the signs
say — & they're
right!

August 2000 .
Entertainment for the queue . . . .
Bubbles & sweets for the children .
Masses of people wanting to see the .
biggest building site in Cornwall

3

I really loved the biomes when you could see the construction of them, layer on layer, r now they look as if they've been covered with giant bubble wrap.

But as I watch, the light changes & the 'bubbles' catch the light & shade. In some places I can see through a little to the construction underneath. The light glows along the tops & shines against a dark sky. The colours change through greys & blues to warmer, yellowy highlights. I've changed my mind - they're still weird & beautiful.

of course it isn't always sunny but they're
ready for every eventuality

6

looking back to the Visitor centre perched on
the edge...

waiting for the 'land-train'
hard hats & yellow jackets —
To get a closer glimpse of the
biomes.

eden p

7

By the beginning of october the big biome is completely covered, waiting for the first trees to arrive.

This will eventually be the main entrance to the Biomes.

But the men are still working in a sea of mud... what looks like a huge, circular puddle is - I think - the start of the amphitheatre.

9

my lorry delivering trees today has got stuck in the mud
and to be towed out by one of the tracked vehicles.
Mud & water everywhere.

My first visit to the large biome. How can I explain the HUGENESS? The feeling of space? It's like stepping inside a cathedral, but one made of light, not stone....

12

's an enormous area of contained light
inted blue by the shadows of trees outside
on the rim of the quarry.

e two pages don't actually fit together —
need a book twice as wide to do that....
ll have to stand at this spot — I think it may be a mangrove swamp! —
understand the vastness.

There are patterns at the
centre of each dome —
Air vents which look like
lotus flowers when
they're open...

13

Men, still at work all over the inside, are they builders who can absiel (I don't think that's the right spelling) or abseilers (is that it?) who can build!

14

* I have found out that they're 'Specialists'. It makes me dizzy just to watch them.

15

furry stems r leaves
elegant

Sanchezia Nobilis

Lantana

Tibouchina urvilleana

Camellia Sno
sij
small, waxy
flowers

malvaviscus arboreus
sprawling out of its pots

Ananus cosmosus

16

flowers at Watering Lane — on a wet & grey october day

Acalypha hispida

Solanum quitoensis,
Huge leaves, hairy & spiky
stems, small hairy flowers
& an orange, hairy
fruit

These wonderful pink flowers are
between 12 - 24" long.

They look artificial.

This is an impatiens with
a very long name . . .
or 'congo cockatoo'!

17

The green hats are gardeners - I'm wearing a white one, so maybe they're for visitors? And I've no idea who wears the red, yellow & blue!

19

It's winter outside!
but it's HOT in here....

21

Men at Work ·

thinking ·

22 planning ·

& even, sometimes, time to pose!

...nting. The orange colour behind is a material which covers some of the slopes. it will be planted through & eventually rot away. (very useful in my pictures!)

23

swinging trees carefully into place –

A huge crane is working inside (r dwarfed by ..) the big biome ..

couldn't find the label on this one
it looks like an ordinary daisy. flowes
with variegated
leaves....

Hibiscus storkii

Canna Indica

Plumeria obtusa
thick, waxy petals twistup in
a spiral from the centre.

26

The Buddha's hand citrus — only restor drawing if there is blossom as well as fruit.

blossom on the orange & lemon trees — so many different sorts — & limes too

This is one of the first big trees to be planted

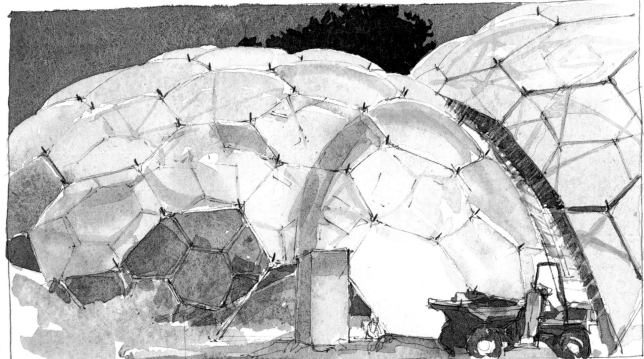

30

31

And outside — it's still raining . . . . . There have only been a few dry days in the last 3 months! In fact it's been the wettest winter since records began . . . And it looks like they're still on schedule!

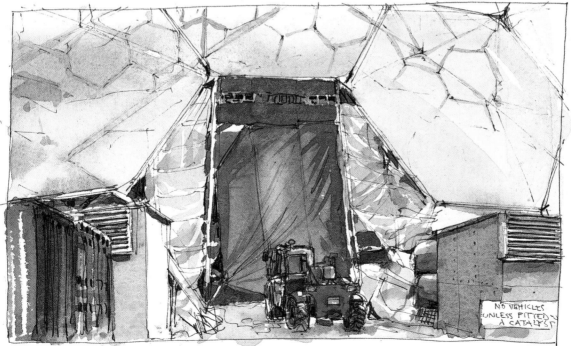

NO VEHICLES
UNLESS FITTED
A CATALYST

33

A friends evening in January — the tenth... & last — lots of laughs & information — very thought provoking — A quote from a friend — "Eden is planting ideas as well as seeds..."

And, after the mulled wine & pasties, a trip down into the big biome. - Lit with coloured spotlights, leaving great areas of darkness

35

Approaching the biomes from the service entrance
A view I've never seen before

his is what you see when you enter the big tropics biome...
raight across the huge space is the 'cliff' on the other side. A
aterfall will cascade from the very top (not in action yet...)
rees have already covered most of the bare slopes.

37

the 'jungle' atmosphere is growing quickly. It's hard to believe that this was an empty space just a couple of months ago.
A 'Longhouse' is going up somewhere in the lower jungle... And the building below is a 'cooling room' for people who find the heat & humidity too much... What a good idea. I think I'll be making use of it.

38.

I keep thinking back to the feeling of space in here the first time I came in when it was empty. Now that it's filling up with trees it feels quite different.

they are beautiful, & it feels crowded & 'jungley' but you look down at them instead of up. That vast space has gone for good..

41

.. But this is what's really exciting

42 plantations of trees & undergrowth

cocoa, I think

looking as if they've been
growing here for years...
everywhere, gardeners, half hidden—
still planting.

43

some of the gardeners were taught to
abseil to plant these steep slopes
by the waterfall. which will be
a wonderful sight when it's flowing
over these boulders & down into the pool at the bottom.

45

46

found these old friends from the watering lane Nursery in the
small lozanne.

47

The Biomes at night - a last view - coloured lights,
tree shadows - r puddles r pools reflecting it all . . . . . . -